Copyright

So, You Want To Be A Nanny?

Publisher Assistant: Nina Motivates LLC

www.ninaaddison.com

publishernina@gmail.com

ISBN: 979-8-9864595-9-2

This Book Belongs To

_____

Acknowledgements

Natasha touched so many lives. Her legacy lives in and through us. Here are some of the names of her loved ones and friends. There are many more names that are not listed but are not forgotten about.

Linda Smith (John) - Natasha's Mother
Chris Ross (Robin - Fiancé) - Natasha's brother
Louisa Francis - Natasha's grandma
Carmen Wallace (James) - Natasha's aunt
Jeromie, Carmen, Jordan, Jeromie JR., Regan, Jayden, and Ryan Shoulders - Natasha's cousins
Keith, Rochelle, Morgan, Avery, and Mia Naylor - Natasha's cousins
Rickelle, Khiry, Kwame, Kensy, and Kyle Couch - Natasha's cousins
Sharon Simmons - Natasha's play Aunt and friend
Mary Pam - Natasha's friend
Pearl, Lili, Shira and Adam McKay - Natasha's former employer and friend
Zipporah Annie Madison (Philip) - Natasha's friend
Justin, Danielle, Vera, Lura, Eden, and Levi Goll - Natasha's friends,
Pastor Jimmy and family Reyes - Natasha's pastor
Cheryl Allen - Natasha's friend
Rebecca Ann Skura - Natasha's friend
Rachael Skura, Stephen Skura - Natasha's friend
Mindy Roh - Natasha's friend
Mandy and Aki Kawamata - Natasha's friend

Caroline Von Petzholdt - Natasha's friend
David Randle - Natasha's friend
Susan Highleyman - Natasha's coach and friend
AB, LB, MB, & ZB - Natasha's friends
Ajay Samuel - Natasha's friend
Aaron and Jamila Jenkins - Natasha's friend
Tristan McCormick, Jasmine McCormick, Deandre
Kelly Saige Powell - Natasha's friends.

Table of Content

Introduction

What would be the most valuable assets you would love to bring to a family that is priceless to everyone? This is an important thing to ask yourself before you begin.

Everyone is great at something, and you bring a part of you to every job. A nanny should bring a spirit of excellence to every job that they take. You want to be set apart from the ordinary nanny and bring something to the table that can is irreplaceable. You are to always bring something new because the job would grow stale if you don't. When you bring that spirit of excellence to your nanny job, you would see it not only benefits your family but will see yourself and the children thriving.

A warning to all nannies, DON'T ENTER A JOB WITH A PASSIVE MENTALITY. Having a passive mentality will set the stage for your voice not to be heard which will be frustrating and can make one feel obsolete in the family?

SO, YOU WANT TO BE A NANNY?

What is my mission?

I want this book to give you the necessary tools to be the best nanny you can be. Not every nanny is suited for every family and that is okay. Think of your skills, your knowledge, and your personality as a craft.

Each family is different and as you work and learn about your employer's family you will naturally develop new knowledge and skills that are suited to that particular family. This will help you to become a valuable asset. Remember that everything you bring to the table is valuable. Unfortunately, many nannies in the childcare industry see their job as a simply a paycheck – a means to an end but being a nanny can become a wonderfully fulfilling lifelong career.

First, some basics:

What is the difference between a mother's helper, babysitter, an au pair, and a nanny?

Mother's Helper

One good option for those people just starting out in the childcare industry is to apply for a "mother's helper" position. A mother's helper is someone who assists with the chores and cares for the children while the mother (or father) are also at home.

Babysitter

A babysitter is the person who is called upon when mom and dad want to go out for a date night for a couple hours, when mom or dad need to run errands or work for a few hours during the day. Typically, a babysitter will work only a couple of times a week.

Au Pair

An au pair is a young foreign person, typically a woman, who lives in with the family and helps with housework or childcare. An au pair must obtain a special visa from their home country and the US.

Nanny

One mom put it this way: The nanny is a surrogate parent. When mom or dad is unable to be there, the nanny is in charge. A nanny will usually be expected to run the household, when the parents are away. A nanny is more likely to have a part-time or full-time work schedule.

A nanny will wear many hats throughout the workday. In addition to nurturing the children's emotional and intellectual development of the children, typical nanny duties may include things like picking the children up from school and driving them to any afterschool activities, helping the children with homework and communicating with the teachers at school. The nanny will be responsible to enforce the household rules and provide appropriate discipline, as modeled by the parents. A nanny may also be required to help keep the children's belongings clean and tidy and provide healthy snacks or meals.

Live in nanny:

A live-in nanny is just what it sounds like: a nanny who lives in the home with her employer's family. Live-in nannies should have their own room and living area. Clear boundaries and expectations are key for working as a thriving and happy live-in nanny. You and your boss should set clear guidelines for when you are working and when you are on your own time. These boundaries and guidelines may evolve over time so it's key to keep communication open with the family.

Your boss will also likely set out ground rules for what is acceptable behavior during your off time. For example, will overnight houseguests, such as a boyfriend or girlfriend) be allowed? How does your boss feel about smoking or alcohol use once you are off work? What rooms are shared and what rooms are off limits when you are not working? Which household items (such as toilet paper, laundry soap, etc.) will the nanny be required to purchase for her own use?

Getting Started

Questions to ask yourself:

Knowing what you want is the first step towards getting what you want. These are the questions you need to ask yourself before you step in to an agency's office or before you apply for independent nanny jobs.

1. What age group do you want to work with? Do you like babies? Are you more comfortable with older children? Are toddlers your favorite age? This should be a priority when seeking a position in childcare. Knowing what age group you are comfortable with will help you to determine which position would be suitable for you. It is wonderful having a job with the age group you prefer because you can really be happy and devoted to the child in your care. Working with children who may be outside your preferred age range can make any nanny job more trying.

There are many jobs that are suitable for people who are simply looking for a paycheck, but a nanny job is not one of them.

2. Are you looking for part time or full-time position as a nanny?

Nannies work all different hours of the day. Each family will require a slightly different schedule. Do you prefer working in the mornings or afternoons? Do you need certain days off each week? Are you okay with working in the evenings?

You may not be able to land a job with the perfect hours right off the bat, but make sure that your job doesn't conflict with any other goals or requirements you have in your life, such as school or family commitments. If you have the time to wait for the precise job to come along then wait, but if not then take something close to the hours that you desire.

3. What is your motivation for becoming a nanny? Do you simply need a paycheck? Are you looking to gain experience for a career in child psychology? Do you think that being a nanny will prepare you to have your own children someday?

Being a nanny is not for the faint of heart. If you are simply looking for an "easy paycheck" then you'd better reconsider and go and get a job doing something else.

It is important not to just take a position just merely for the money and not get the age group you want. Yes, the money sounds great, but your motives need to be in the right place. The age group you have chosen has to be a match and not more than you can handle. If the only true motive which will keep you going is money, it will not seem appealing as time goes on. You must be devoted to your job and putting your best foot forward. When your heart is not in it the parents are likely to see that and would likely let you go. You want a job where you can make a difference, a job where you can be an asset to the family.

4. How is your driving record?

Simply put – most agencies won't accept you if you have serious violations (such as a DUI, reckless driving or many speeding tickets) on your driving record. Most parents will insist on a nanny with a clean driving record.

Most agencies are looking for nannies with at least two years of experience.

Where to find a family?

If you are new to the childcare industry your best bet may be to find a family through job match websites such as care.com, nannies4hire.com or craigslist. Some families still advertise in the local newspaper or with community board notices.

Going with a nanny agency:

The more traditional way of finding a family is to go through an agency. Nanny agencies charge a fee to the family that is looking for help. This fee typically comes with a guarantee that the nanny they find will be a great fit. If the nanny leaves or is fired during the first three months of employment the agency is responsible for finding another nanny for free of charge. Because of this some nanny agencies have the reputation of putting the needs of the family first and not caring about the needs of the nanny. But not all nanny agencies are created equal. Do your research and go with an agency that will strive to meet the needs of both the family and the nanny.

For a nanny with experience the better choice is an agency. There are benefits of going through an agency. Most agencies are looking for nannies with at least two years of experience.

You will interview with the agency before you interview with a family. You can expect the agency to ask you a variety of questions about yourself, your hobbies and why you want to work with children. The agency will also ask about job specifics such as the hours you want to work and what kind of salary and benefits you require. It is to your benefit to have a dedicated point of contact within the agency.

Your agency should break down your role in the family.

2. What should you wear for an interview with an agency or family?

There is a saying: the first impression is the last impression. Let me tell you: The family wants to see Mary Poppins when they open the door to you.

Ladies:

- Dress conservatively.
- Pants should fit well and not be too tight or too baggy. Skip the blue jeans and opt for more tailored slacks.
- Skirts and dresses should be at or near knee length.
- Tops should be modest and elegant.
- Shoes should have low or flat heels. Make sure your shoes will allow you to get down to the child's level when you first meet them.
- Little or no perfume. Remember that some children may be sensitive to certain scents.
- Neat and tidy hairstyle

- Tasteful jewelry, no long or dangling earrings!
- Natural looking make-up

Men:

- Dress conservatively.
- Pants should fit well and not be too tight or too baggy. Skip the blue jeans and opt for more tailored slacks.
- Wear a clean and pressed polo or button up shirt
- Shoes should be nice looking – no ratty sneakers please!
- Little or no cologne – remember that some children may be sensitive to certain scents.
- Neat and tidy hairstyle.
- If you wear jewelry, please make sure it is tasteful. Keep jewelry to a minimum.

3. How do you interview with the family?

Be punctual!

Bring an extra copy of your references and resume as well as your identifying documents such as your driver's license, and social security card or birth certificate. Bring copies of your letters of recommendation as well as any certifications you hold (First Aid, CPR, etc.).

Even though you may feel like you have your interview questions memorized, bring a copy of them.

The most important thing you can bring to an interview is confidence in your knowledge and experience. Your confidence will help put the parents at ease and demonstrate that they can feel safe leaving their precious children in your care.

Familiarize yourself with the job that you are applying for.

Have some examples for them. If they need flexibility then show and tell them how flexible you are. For instance, my evenings are free if you need extra care etc.

Listen, listen, listen to what they are asking for and ask yourself is this the house you want to come to every day, is there comfortable feeling that you are getting with the mom and the children?

Things you may be asked during your interview:

What do you like about being a nanny? (Or, if this is your first experience, why do you want to be a nanny?)

How long did you work for your previous family, what were your duties, and why did you leave?

This is the time to dazzle the family with all your accomplishments, relevant skills, and unique experiences.

Familiarize yourself with the job that you are applying for.

Listen carefully to what the parents are saying and ask yourself honestly: Can I see myself coming here every day to care for their children? Would I feel comfortable in this house and with these people?

Questions to ask the family:

Don't be shy! Many nannies think it's polite not to ask anything during an interview, but you really want to show the family that you have thought through the job.

1. Ask specific questions about the temperament of the children. Listen as the parents describe their children. Are the kids shy? Feisty? Spirited? Bookish? Playful? Serious?

2. Is there any medication that will need to be administered on a daily basis?

3. Ask the parents to describe the ideal daily schedule. Make sure you find out about school pick up times, after school activities, evening schedules, and bedtime routines.

4. Will you be required to drive the children around on a regular basis? And if so, will you be using your own car, or will the family provide a car for you to use? If you will be using your own car, be sure to inquire about gasoline reimbursement.

5. Are there expectations of any additional duties such as cooking or light housekeeping?

7. What type of snacks will be permitted during the day? Does the family have any dietary restrictions?

8. Will you be expected to help with homework depending on the ages of the children?

9. What kind of discipline is used in the house? What kind of discipline will you be asked to use with the children?

10. The last question to ask about is compensation.

If the interview has been conducted at the family home, it is appropriate to ask to see the children's rooms. Pay attention to the room - it will give you insight. For example, if the children's rooms are full with books you can surmise that the parent encourages reading and perhaps is very active in reading to the child. You could assume that you would be expected to follow this example. Likewise, if the child's room is very tidy it's a likely assumption that you will be expected to help keep it that way.

Congratulations! You've got the job. Now what?

Get It In Writing or That Legalese Contract Stuff

If you have been hired through an agency, then the agency can negotiate many of these details for you. However, it is wise to double check with the family to make sure that there is no misinformation regarding your contract. Additionally, some agencies will allow you to negotiate with the family directly.

Some nannies are comfortable with a simple verbal contract – but it is in your best interest to have a basic contract written up. It doesn't have to be elaborate, but it should contain information about the following items:

Your start date

Weekly work schedule and hours

Salary

Annual review process and raises

Benefits

Vacation and Holidays

A note about vacations and holidays:

Two weeks paid vacation per year is standard. Keep in mind that your vacation doesn't need to happen at the same time that the family takes their own vacation. The family could be planning to go on a trip for the month of June and your vacation plans could be in the month of February.

It may be tempting for your employer to encourage you to take your vacation congruent to the family's vacation. After all, your employer may not like the idea of paying your salary when you are not working. However, by continuing to employ you while they are out of town ensures that you will still be available to work (and haven't had to go find another job) when they return.

Not all holidays are paid time off. You should negotiate with the family ahead of time to determine which holidays you will work and which you will have off. If you work on a federal holiday you are entitled to time and a half pay. These holidays include special days like Memorial Day, July 4th, Thanksgiving, Christmas, and New Years Day.

What happens when you take your vacation? Is it your responsibility to find someone to cover your shift?

Planning your vacation? While it is not required for you to take your vacation at the same time as your employer, it is reasonable to negotiate the timing of your vacation. Your boss may ask you to not schedule time off during a particularly busy week or season, such as the beginning of the school year.

A good rule of thumb is to give your employer two months' notice about your plans (and remind your boss again at one month and two weeks out from your vacation). This gives your employer plenty of time to search for a nanny to replace you while you are away. It is not your responsibility to find a temporary nanny or babysitter. Your employer may be able to call your agency for a replacement. However, if you know of a nanny that would be a good fit while you are gone then, by all means, introduce him or her to your employer. Your boss will greatly appreciate the recommendation.

You will need to have the substitute nanny shadow you at work for a day or two so that they learn the routine and get to know the children a little bit. It would also be helpful to write out a schedule with the relevant times and addresses that the substitute would need. You should set the substitute nanny up for success – that way you can relax and not worry if your employer is being taken care of while you are away.

Paid Sick days

Most employees can expect an average of five to eight paid sick days per year. Alternatively, some employers call these days "Paid Personal Days" which means that the employee can use them for any number of reasons including family emergencies, scheduling personal appointments such as doctor visits or simply for a day of much needed rest.

Healthcare benefits:

Unfortunately, because the healthcare industry is changing so rapidly in the U.S. right now it's nearly impossible to speak with authority on this topic at this time. If you are not going through an agency, make sure to check with your state's healthcare requirements for small businesses with domestic workers. Be informed and know your rights.

Do a paid week trial.

It's important to insist on a paid week trial. If possible, the trial period should include the full scope of the nanny duties, including any driving, errands, cooking, housework or any other activities that would go on in a normal week. Not only will this give you a good idea about the schedule and expectations of the family, but you will be able to get to know the parents and children better.

A trial period is beneficial to both the nanny and the parent. Remember: while you are scoping out the family, they are checking you out to see if you are a good fit with their children and lifestyle. If, on the off chance, you decide that the job or family isn't the right fit for you then at least you'll know that it's time to move on before you commit yourself any further to that family.

Day-to-Day Nanny tips:

Time management/Being on time

Being on time to work shows that you are serious about your job, it shows professionalism and points to your character.

A note about arriving late for work: or the dreaded "the alarm didn't go off" scenario…

Example: You wake up late. You missed the alarm! Don't wait until the parent calls you – reach out and call them first if you are anticipating a problem. Your employer might be angry, but it's better to address the situation head on. Don't explain your tardiness on the phone and don't explain as you walk through the door. Wait until the day is over and then apologize and explain what you are going to do in the future to make sure you are not late anymore. Your boss may want to express her disappointment. Let her talk and don't interrupt. When she is finished simply apologize and let her know how you will strive to be on time or early in the future. A good suggestion is to tell them that you are going to be fifteen or thirty minutes early from now on.

In the same way, if you are running late to take the children to an appointment – such as a doctor's visit – make sure you call the facility yourself to let them know you are on your way. That will prevent the facility from bothering your boss at work.

Out and about with children: what is in your car and purse?

Spare Clothes

Kids are messy! A good nanny will have at least one change of clothes per child in their car. Make sure to update these clothes as the seasons change (and toss in a bottle of sunscreen!). An exceptional nanny will also keep one fancy outfit per child in their car. Why? You never know when the parents may come up with some last-minute plans (or they forgot to tell you the plans) that require fancy dress for the children.

First Aid Kit

A small first aid kit in your purse or bag is essential. You should also keep a larger, more complete first aid kit in your car. A small first aid kit should include baby or children Tylenol or Advil, bandages (children colorful bandages with fun pictures on them are always a fun idea) and an antibiotic cream such as Neosporin. It's also smart to have some medication in your kit for adults. You never know when you may run into another nanny or mother on the playground with a headache. You will feel good to be able to offer them Tylenol or Advil. Ladies: you may also want to add a few feminine products to your kit in case they are needed.

A note about giving medication to children:

Make sure you know ahead of time if the parent would like to be notified before any medication is administered to their child. If in doubt, always contact the parent before you give any mediation to their child.

Water or juice and snacks:

This is especially a good idea for nannies of toddlers and younger children. Having a sippy cup of water or juice plus some simple snacks (like crackers or fruit) can help keep a temper tantrum at bay if the errands go longer than expected.

Other tips:

Be organized:

Write down the week's schedule ahead of time and include any relevant phone number or addresses you'll need that week (such as play date information or doctor's appointments). You can use a day planner or notebook, or you can use your phone or tablet. This planning and forethought will impress your employer.

Driving on the job:

Every nanny that is using their own car during work should keep a mileage log and be compensated for gasoline and mileage on a weekly or monthly basis. You may also want to discuss partial reimbursement for other miscellaneous expenses such as car washes, oil changes, and new tires as you will be required to perform more frequent maintenance on your car if you are using it for work.

Insurance:

Check to see if your current car insurance covers passengers in your vehicle. The parents will be responsible for taking out additional insurance to cover their children if need be.

How to earn respect from the children

1. Trust

It has been said trust is not given but it is earned; respect must be demanded. The definition of respect is a feeling of deep admiration for someone, or something elicited by their abilities, qualities or achievements.

2. Appropriate and consistent boundaries

Boundary (A line that marks the limits of an area, a dividing line). All children desire boundaries even though they don't know it. Teaching children boundaries when they are young will help them into adulthood. One might wonder what respect has to do with boundaries? The two are entwined. By having healthy boundaries, one learns to respect everyone and their property. Disrespect happens when boundaries are broken which then can lead to some negative consequences.

When a new addition is added to a family which is YOU the nanny, you might feel like one is tipping their toe in un-chartered territory, but it is then, you as the nanny needs to stand your ground and sets a precedent not only for the time you are there but hopefully for the rest of the children's lives. Children will always test boundaries which is what they do best. They want to see how much they can get away and how far they can go. It will usually start the first day that you begin, for example the common phrase, (MOM LETS ME DO THIS). Now some nannies could or maybe believe this cute innocent child standing before them but the best thing to do in this moment is tell the child in a very stern voice to stop what they are doing. Then tell them that you will call their parents to eliminate any confusion. When children know you mean business they start to whip into shape, they realize you are fun but not to cross you and a level of respect is born.

Teaching responsibility: How to teach children responsibilities around the house.

This issue is a big one; the parents really need to be on board with you. Teaching a child responsibilities need to be implemented at a young age. It can start with little things such as when they come into the house and take off their shoes to put them by the stairs. When they come home from school not to throw their school bag in front of the hallway or leave it in a place where someone could trip or fall but place it in a safe place. As they get older different responsibilities will be asked of them. It might feel like nagging because you are asking them over and over again to do the same thing. Have a little patience because in the beginning they might forget but in time it will become second nature to them. As a nanny there is so much you can do Monday through Friday that is why this is a team effort with your boss to continue this process over the weekend what has been started.

How to be on the same page as your boss concerning the children.

It is frustrating and disrespectful if a parent overrides your authority in front of the children or behind your back, especially when the parent has given you that same authority to be exercised towards her children. In order to have a successful working relationship with the family the parents must trust you to raise their children in their absence. That trust will come through frequent communication and demonstrations of

respect. As a nanny, you should request to have a meeting with your employer every two to four weeks. This regular meeting time will be especially key for nannies who live-in with their employer. These meetings do not have to be long and formal, but nanny and parent should talk about what is going well and what needs to be improved. This is also a time to make sure you are presenting a united front with the parents towards the children. Just as you would not want the parents to undermine your authority – neither should you allow behavior or activities that the parents do not approve of. It is your job to reinforce what the parents are already teaching and modeling, whether or not you agree with every decision that the parents make.

Another item to discuss is how often do the parents want to be contacted during the day? For example, when you pick up the children from school should you check in with the parents to see what the plan for the rest of the day is? Do the parents want you to send any fun photos or updates from their children to help them keep in touch?

Another good communication method is to take five minutes each day as you end work to discuss the next day's activities.

Pick a project which you will focus on with the kids every year.

Talk to the parents about it so they are on board. It will show them that you want to improve the quality of their lives as well as their children. Make sure chores are done and suggest an incentive board. Help them with their school assignments, particularly in areas that you are gifted in. This is an opportunity to improve your relationship with the children.

CPR Certification

Every nanny should be trained in infant and child CPR. Some agencies require a current training or certification before they will place you with a family. Most local hospitals and the Red Cross offer workshops and classes in CPR and basic first aid.

Is it a requirement that you know how to cook?

Even if cooking meals is not in your job description it is a good idea to be able to cook a few basic meals. There may be a time when your employer gets stuck at work or is running late, and you may need to stay late and prepare dinner for the children. You don't have to be a gourmet chef, but knowledge of a few basic cooking skills and some simple, healthy (and child-friendly) recipes will make you a valuable asset to your employer.

Preserve the privacy of your employer.

Keep your job and the children out of your social media posts. Every nanny has spontaneous moments to take cute pictures or capture silly moments but remember that these are not your children. At the very least, please make sure to ask for the parent's permission before you post something to social media.

Limit your usage of screen time, including phone calls, texting, and tablet use.

Remember that you are not on your own time – you are working. Schedule time to make personal phone calls and communicate with your friends and family after you are off work. Your phone should not interfere with your time on the job.

Pro Tip: Get a letter of reference every year.

Special circumstances:

Traveling with the family

Staying overnight with the family

How to ask for a raise

New baby in the family

Traveling with your employer or "Is this really a vacation?"

Some families want their nanny to travel with them when they go on vacation. While you will still be working and watching the children, you may also have wonderful opportunities to taste local cuisine, visit world-class museums, and spend time sightseeing with your children in tow.

But before you pack your bags, you'll need to make sure you cover some of the basics with your family about pay and hours. You'll need to remember that while it is a vacation for the family it is not a vacation for you, the nanny.

If you work thirty to forty hours per week for your family when they are at home be aware that you will probably be working more hours when you are on vacation with them. Instead of an eight-hour day with the family you may be working up to twelve hours per day. It's wise to assume that you'll be taking care of the children from the moment they wake up in the morning until they go to sleep at night. This extra time could possibly include cooking the children breakfast, lunch, and dinner.

Therefore, it's imperative to sit down with your boss before the trip and discuss the additional hours that you will be working. It is beneficial to both the family and the nanny if you can come up with an outline of a daily schedule and agree upon how much extra money you will be paid for working additional hours.

Preparing for the Trip

It is very likely it will be your responsibility to pack for the children. Make yourself a detailed checklist and get started gathering and packing key items at least a week ahead of the trip. Packing earlier allows you to free your mind to remember all the last-minute details and items that were left off your list.

Pro tip: pack a special activities bag for the airplane. A brand-new coloring book, a new set of crayons, a special sticker book or a couple of new toy cars will make the child feel like the time stuck on the plane is fun and exciting. Pack some of their old favorite toys as well. Having a well-stocked "goodie bag" will help keep boredom at bay.

Staying overnight with the family.

Parents sometimes must go out of town for a day or a weekend and will ask their nanny to stay overnight with their children. It's wise to discuss the additional pay before the overnight stay. You can either agree to a fixed price for the overnight work, or you could calculate your pay as half your hourly rate during the hours when the children are asleep.

New baby in the family or "Was that the sound of my workload doubling?"

Simply stated, if you will be taking care of the new baby in addition to your other duties then your pay should be adjusted appropriately. This should not be an area of compromise. If your employer does not want to increase your salary according to the number of children you will be taking care of then, unfortunately, you should look for a new family.

How to ask for a raise.

Asking for a raise can be intimidating, especially in an employment situation where you, the nanny, are part of a household. It can be easy to think of yourself as a member of the family and not as an employee. You need to remember that the parents you work for are like the employers of a business and it might help you overcome some of your hesitancy about asking for a raise.

If you weren't able to include an annual raise in your employment contract there are a few things you should do before you sit down and ask for a raise.

1. Do a self-evaluation. Be honest with yourself about your abilities, any challenges you've dealt with in the past year, and ways in which you've been an asset to the family. Ask yourself: Did I struggle with tardiness? Have I been available to pick up extra hours or stay later to help out when needed? Have you picked up any extra responsibilities for the family since your last raise? How have I gone above and beyond for the family?

Write down some examples to help you during your discussion with your employer.

2. Consider how much of a raise you desire and come up with a specific number or percentage increase. Think about how your average cost-of-living expenses may have gone up in the last year. Things like rent, food, and insurance tend to become more expensive every year, so factor those things into your equation. Be prepared with a range of numbers that may be acceptable to you. Your employer might be willing to give you a raise, but they may want to negotiate the amount. If you would like a five percent raise but you would settle for a three percent raise keep that in mind.

3. Do some research to find out how much nannies make in your area. If you are making a below average wage compared to your nanny peers, you can consider mentioning that when you speak to your employer.

When you have completed your prep work, you're ready to sit down with your employer and discuss a raise. Don't spring the topic on them at the spur of the moment but ask them if you could have fifteen or twenty minutes of their time sometime in the next few days to discuss your employment.

During the conversation:

1.   Let your employer know how much you enjoy working for them.

2.   Tell them you've done a self-evaluation and wanted to get any feedback from them. Share your examples of how you've been an asset to the family and remind them of any extra responsibilities you've taken on for the family recently. Ask them if there is anything you can improve on.

If your employer says yes:

1.   Thank them!

2.   Tell them you think an annual (or bi-annual) review process is helpful and suggest that you schedule another conversation in six months or a year.

3.   Update your contract (it's a good idea to have both parties initial a note stating the amount of the raise and the date).

If your employer says no:

1.   Find out if there is anything you are doing that is preventing you from getting a raise.

2.   Ask them if you can revisit the topic in three months (perhaps the family finances are tight right

now, but they would be able to give you a raise in the near future).

Here is the tough part: you need to be willing to leave your job if your employer says no to your raise or if you feel they are being unreasonable. The hard truth is that some families will have no intention of giving a raise to the nanny. If this is your case, then your best course of action is to ask for a current reference letter from your employer. You can let them know that you will need to start looking for a second job to make ends me, or you can tell them that you will be looking for a new nanny position with another family because your finances dictate that you need to make more money. Sometimes the prospect of losing you, a valuable member of their household, may be enough for your employer to agree to a raise. But be careful! Don't make this announcement unless you are ready and willing to follow up with looking for a new or second job.

Note: It's sad to say, but often if a nanny has been with a family for many years without a pay raise the family may be the type that does not consider it reasonable to give raises to household help. If you have been with the family for more than three years without a raise, then your request may lead to a more difficult conversation. Though, on the other hand, your employer may realize that a raise is long overdue and may readily agree to increase your salary.

Working for a challenging employer

You will learn a lot by working for a challenging employer. While it will not always be easy, and you may be tempted to give up, in the long run you will learn many valuable lessons by dealing with difficult people and meeting high expectations. Of course, you should never stay with an employer that is in any way abusive.

Challenge yourself to exceed their high demands! If your employer wants to you start work at nine o'clock, arrive fifteen to thirty minutes early.

Another benefit of working for a challenging boss is that after a while you will learn valuable people skills that will be their own reward. You will become the nanny that is able to please every family and an agency will be able to place you with a job that no one else could handle.

Pro-Tip: Be one step ahead. Have a vision for your work with the children.

Are the kids getting out of school for the summer soon? Present your employer with a list of potential summer activities you'd like to do with the children (museums, art projects, summer classes, reading lists, etc.) the month before school get out.

Moving on.

When to leave the family

Giving notice

Keeping in touch

Nanny McPhee movie:

"There is something you should understand about the way I work. When you need me but do not want me, then I must stay. When you want me but no longer need me, then I have to go. It's rather sad, really, but there it is."

When to move on from your family.

This can be a complicated question. There is no easy answer, and the timeline will vary from person to person, job to job. Consider your own goals and the needs of the family.

Start putting feelers out for a new family when you know that you've got about 2 years left.

One is at the age worrying about their future as a nanny, is it a job or can it take you into various departments of the childcare industry which you can make it a career.

It can feel like there is no easy or right time to leave the family. There are many emotions one goes through when deciding it is time to leave. There could be feelings of injustice with the job. You may have feelings that it is time to move on to bigger and better things as a new career path. You may want to move on with a different family working with a baby, because the children you have been taking care of throughout years are all grown up and you feel your services are not needed or you are bored with your job and need something new. Whatever the case may be, emotions of feeling guilty can play into it.

The summer is usually the best time to leave while the children are out of school; however, if the summer is too long it is better if you leave before school next semester starts. A good time could be before the fall while the children are out of school so they can adjust from school studies and your departure. It gives your boss the right amount of time to hire the right nanny for their family.

Finally, don't stay with a family that leaves you constantly frustrated or bored to tears. You should look for a new position before you get to the point where you want to throw the towel in.

Giving notice (how much time)

This particular question varies depending on how long you have been with the family. If you have been with the family for less than one year, then a two weeks' notice is usually sufficient. If you have been with the family for many years, then it is advisable to give up to three months' notice. This extended time will allow the children to adjust to the idea of a new nanny and will give the parents plenty of time to interview and hire someone else.

The children should be your first priority when you are planning on leaving a family. Children can form very strong emotional bonds with their nanny, especially if the nanny has been with them for many years. Take care to explain to the child that it is not their fault that you are leaving. You can help prepare the children for the upcoming changes and help facilitate a smooth transition.

Keeping in touch once you've left the family.

Is it wise after you have left the family to keep in touch?

After a job has ended, you should not feel obligated to keep in touch. However, assuming you left on good terms, most families would be happy to have a phone call or quick visit from you.

Don't worry that you will step on the toes of the new nanny by keeping in touch with the children. The children will miss you and knowing you are just a phone call away can help with the transition.

Another good reason for keeping in touch is that the parents can always call you if they need an occasional babysitter. The children would love to have their favorite nanny to babysit them.

Pay raise

There are several steps one can take to put this outward issue into motion to make it less scary, now I am not saying this will guarantee this will give you a raise but it will give you a starting point.

1.Try to include it in your contract.

2. Ask your employer are you free to discuss a pay raise.

2. Do a self-evaluation.

3. Ask the parent if there is anything you can improve on and if so what is it.

4. Is there more responsibility you would like me to take on.

5. Is there anything that can prevent from me getting my raise?

6. How much of a raise do you need?

7. Are you ready to leave? If they say NO, are you being reasonable.

For someone who has been on a job for a short period of time like a year compared to a nanny who has been with a family more than a year, typically a raise is in order. The truth is for the nannies who have been with a family for over three years or so and has not receive a raise, this family has no intention of giving you one it is as plain and simple. It is hard to pill to swallow I know, the truth is when a family realize that you are amazing part or even part of their family, they don't want to lose you, they know you are valuable and if they can see it then someone else can too, so they will try to accommodate you in whatever you need of course in reason.

If you are that nanny who has been with a family for a while and have not receive a raise, all is not lost, the recommended thing to do is to ask your employer for reference because you are looking for a part time job so at least you have a reference from them and start looking for another job if you feel if you ask for a raise you would be denied. Another turn in events could happen you decided to leave give your notice and it is then they realize they don't want to lose you and offer you more money but that is gamble it might work in your favor or not.

For the Parents

How to pick the right nanny

1A) Where and how to find a nanny? There are many options for finding quality childcare. Websites such as care.com are dedicated to matching nannies and babysitters to families. Other parents have had luck placing an ad on websites like craigslist.org or even looking through the newspaper classifieds.

The traditional way to find a nanny is to go through an agency. Agencies offer the benefit of doing a lot of the legwork for you. They will screen applicants, do a background check (including their driving record), and thoroughly check their references. A good agency will make sure to match you with a nanny that can work the hours that you require and has the skill set you need for your family. Nanny agencies typically require their applicants to have at least two years of experience working in childcare.

But instead on relying just on the agency finding, one should have their own questions they would love to ask the nanny.

If paying agency fees is not feasible for your family, then it's in your best interest to do your homework and thoroughly check the applicant's references. References can be fraudulent.

Either way, go with your gut. If you feel like something is "off" about a certain applicant trust your instinct and do not hire that person. It's far better to hold out for a better fit for your family than to hire a nanny that you do not trust.

Another great option is to offer your potential nanny a weeklong paid trial in order to get a better feel for their personality and abilities.

A week's trial is for your benefit. You want to see how the child responds to the new nanny and as well as to see if you and new nanny are compatible.

During the week trial, it is wise to pay the nanny as if she has already presumed the positions, whatever fee that is agree upon should be set for the following week, if you choose to hire nanny after the week trial is over for a permanent position for your family.

A week trial helps you to determine if the nanny you have hired is the right fit it also helps you to see if the nanny knows how to interact with children. How does she communicate with them? How does she take your directions on things you tell her? Is she assertive or hangs back and lets the child run the show? Is she polite, is she knowledgeable about baby proofing around the house? Is she the kind of nanny that puts the child in front of the television set while she is doing things around the house? If you are not around that trial week, it will be impossible to know these things. However, if you have the time to be around, little hints will let you know, your gut instincts will tell you if she will be able to work for your family as a nanny or just babysit here or there.

What are the criteria that you are looking for in your nanny?

It is helpful to know exactly what you are looking for before you take that first step before inquiring about childcare.

Here are some things you might what to consider:

Are they able to prepare dinner for the children or the family? What about their personality? Is it fun loving, high energy or down to earth or practical? How do they discipline? Are they laid back, kids will be kids or strict in laying down the rules such as boundaries? Do they have organizational skills, taking notes on what needs to be done throughout the day? Do they know how to organize appointments for afternoon activities? Are they dependent, taking action being assertive? Are they reliable? If you ask them to do something, are they faithful to their word? Are they flexible? If asked to stay late or change their time to come in, are they able to? Also, if you have a pool, would a criteria be for the nanny to know how to swim?

Is an older nanny better than a younger nanny?

Older people may have the experience; however, they might not have the energy with a younger child. A young person might be quicker on the feet and be able to multitask on various activities. A younger person can also be more adaptable and learn from the experience whereas an older person might be set in their own ways in how to raise a child. On the other hand, you might want someone who has experience and knows what to do when a child is sick and to be able to nurse them back to health in your absence. So, someone with years of experience can put your mind to rest, it really depends on your preference.

Should you hire a nanny that is presently in school?

This could be a deal breaker or not at all depending on when/ what you need childcare for. If you need childcare for a couple of hours after school this can be very feasible. Now, depending on the times which you are looking for, the nanny's school hours could interfere with her flexibility to be on call in extreme circumstances. Examples include if the child is sick, and you need your nanny to come in earlier then her original time? It could also be staying later. Another suggestion is to have a back-up babysitter that you can call.

What is their major and how might that apply to their job?

It does not matter what major one is studying for but of course if it's anything to do with child psychology or anything related to children it is a plus, gaining knowledge while working in the field of childcare can be very effective.

How long it will take to complete their degree can determine if that person would be with the family long term. What are their goals once they obtain their degree.

If a nanny is in school studying for a degree that you are considering hiring, it is best to know if you are looking for something part time or long term or maybe you are not sure as of yet, just seeing where things will go for the time being. Most families would love for someone to be around while the kids are growing up depending on the ages of the children. The truth of the matter is if one is going to school and has finished their studies, they would be looking for a job in that particular field, if it is child psychology, they would probably be looking for something in the school system or if their degree is in something else then they would be looking in that field. The good news is usually while they

are looking they would still need a job to pay their daily and monthly expenses, so the search for their dream job would usually take some time.

What about a nanny that can cook?

Finding someone who can cook is a plus in the childcare industry. A nanny specialty is taking care of the children, providing playtime, picking them up from school and being responsible and sweet. However, not many can prepare a meal for a family from scratch but typically can warm up food that is pre- cooked, such as chicken nuggets, fish sticks or making pasta and macaroni cheese for the children. It really depends on your needs, maybe you have someone who prepares meals for your family already or provides dinner in your department when you come home. If you need someone to make dinner for just your little ones, then you may or may not need someone really experienced in the kitchen, but it can be extremely helpful to you.

CPR certified. If you find an applicant that you really like but they are not CPR certified, you can offer to pay for their certification as a condition of being hired. The Red Cross and most local hospitals offer CPR training classes.

Paid vacation

One to two weeks paid vacation is the standard to give to your nanny, depending on the number of years your nanny has been working for you. If your nanny wants to take her vacation in the month of April and your family wants to take theirs in the month of June that should be ok as long as the nanny lets you know ahead of time for you to find someone to cover her shift. It is not the nanny responsibility to find someone to cover her shift. If she has a friend that you know who usually babysits and you as the parent feels comfortable to use them, then asking the nanny if that babysitter is available should be more than efficient.

The family vacation

If the family is going on their vacation and do need the nanny to come along? If so, is the nanny getting paid? One would say if a nanny were on salary, then yes, she automatically gets paid but if one is paid hourly then no. You need to be fair to the nanny because they are an employee and not a family member. When a parent decides to go on a vacation and not take their nanny that is a conscious decision on the parents' part. However, if the nanny is willing and able to work and you don't need her, that is not her fault, so she still needs to be paid for that time.

Paying your nanny while you are gone is like insurance that covers your family in case of an emergency. It is the reassurance that she will be there when you come back, it also shows your nanny that you appreciate her work and that you value her.

Holidays

Holidays are the number one item which is overlooked and missed during the interview process. So how many paid holidays should a nanny receive without having to work? All holidays should be paid, they are traditional holidays which you as the employer gets off.

So, the same should apply to your nanny If you would need your nanny on a particular holiday then paying them time and half pay is mandated by federal law.

Salary: How will you be paying the nanny?

Would it be hourly, or will you be paying on a salary? If you are paying your nanny a salary the hours should be discussed. For example, 30 hours for $700 a week, Monday through Friday or 40 hours for much more and if those hours for any reason do not get fulfilled, they can made up by the following week or by you staying little late or maybe made up through weekend. Whatever is discussed should be written down in a contract and signed by both parties. If paid hourly, it might be wise to have a little note pad or an excel spreadsheet to keep track of the hours throughout the week so you can give the right payout. If you would like your nanny to work on the weekends but they have fulfilled their hours for the week, you could ask as a favor or you can compensate them for the hours you would need them to work at a rate you are probably paying them or little more since it is a day they are usually off.

Should you hire someone who has a degree in childcare versus experience in the field?

Someone with only a degree and little experience would probably make some mothers uncomfortable and on the other hand some mothers would be ok with it. I will tell you no book can really prepare someone to know the inner workings of a child.

When you hire someone with a degree in childcare, they have a vast amount of book knowledge but also having hands on experience gives them a wider scope on things. In the childcare industry, a nanny with experience does know how to distinguish what is good for one child is not necessarily good for another child.

If you are looking for a just a babysitter, it really doesn't matter if they have a lot of an experience but if one is looking for a nanny then experience should outweigh a degree.

Ask about their flexibility.

Flexibility is very important depending on the demand of the job. If you need someone who can be flexible in their schedule that should be the number one priority that is brought up in the interview process before you go any further with the interview. Of course, flexibility differs from one person to the next, but the professional way is to give the same courtesy and respect as you would like to be shown to give the same. Ask your nanny ahead of time so they can rearrange their schedule to accommodate you.

What about nanny cams?

Even with your best judgment of character, it's wise to go with your instincts. Do not to be in any haste to hire someone, even if it might take a while for the hiring process, it is better to be safe than to be sorry.

Every mother has the right to check in to see how their child is being taking care of by the nanny who they have hired in their absence. Some might say a nanny cam is a violation of someone's privacy; that is why if you are thinking of putting up a nanny cam or you have already had one in place it is best to tell the nanny. Some might say why let them know but when someone knows they are being watched they are very careful in their actions, as time goes on, they themselves will forget that the nanny cam is there and go about their typical daily routine.

Important questions to ask.

Did you give the family enough time, such as three weeks or a month, so they could find the right person for the job which would be suited for the children? Did they stay on to offer to train the nanny? Of course, you will be able to validate all the information through speaking with the nanny previous bosses.

What is the nanny short- and long-term goals in their life? The response will show you how they think about the future.

If you are looking for a nanny who will be with your family for the long haul it is best to know what her goals are for the future. Is she looking to be with a family for years to come or something short term to pay bills? Now not everyone really knows where one will be in the next five years but one has a desire to be somewhere or be doing something in the next two years. So, if a nanny tells you they are not sure or has a rough idea for maybe two years, maybe you can express your desire and see if this person is a perfect fit for your family.

Why did you leave your last family and how did you leave them?

This question is vital because it lets you know if you hire them, they will likely do the same actions they did. What you are looking for by asking these questions is a valid reason for their departure. For example, the family moved to another country, or the nanny asked for a pay raise which was well deserved, and they refuse to it give it to her even though they had it or they did not want to compensate in another way. Maybe the children had gotten bigger, and the nanny hours got cut due to the kids being in school all day and their services was not really needed.

How much notice did they give to the family is important?

You want someone who is looking out for the family and especially for the children. No matter what the difference is with the nanny and the family you want to know if that person has integrity to do the right thing. Did they give their former employer the same courtesy which you are hoping for from them?

When do you give a raise and how much?

A raise is usually given based upon the nanny's performance. An evaluation or a performance review should be given by you, the employer, every year to talk about what you are expecting and what improvements you would like to see. You should also express your appreciation for the work the nanny is doing. A pay raise is typically a 3% to 5% increase a year.

Christmas bonuses. How much will you give the first year and the following years going forward?

Bonuses are usually dependent on the boss's generosity but usually the going rate is whatever the nanny is making for a week is given the first year. For the second year it could be the same rate with a $100 more added to the first week pay. Or you could give two weeks' pay the second year, it really depends on you but like I said the standard is what is mentioned above.

What clear guidelines will you provide about cell phones?

As a parent you don't want to tell your nanny that she cannot be on the phone during working hours, it would seem a little bit insensitive especially if there is an emergency or you need to speak to her, so clear guidelines must be discussed. The web which could only be accessed through a stationary internet that needed you to sit down in front of it is more portable than ever, now one can access the web through their phone and for many young people this is their access to the outside world through face-book, twitter, instant gram and many more. Every parent wants to feel that their nanny has their undivided attention on the kids while they are in her care and not mostly on the phone. To alleviate this problem the phone could be used if the children are taking a nap or watching television or when the nanny is taking her lunch break. Also, if they are out and about and you as the parent needs to talk to her is another reason for the phone. So, the phone while the nanny is working should be solely for working purposes or to the incidents mentioned above.

What is a confidentiality agreement?

A confidentiality contract is usually drawn up by the family's lawyer or by the family themselves. The contract has stipulations about what is expected from you. A contract is not always required from a family but for most affluent families it is a way to protect their personal lives from leaking to the outside world. A confidentiality agreement is usually given to the employees who work in the household. That means whatever is privately talked about or seen in the privacy of the home, should NOT be discussed with friends or especially to the tabloids. If the contract is broken for any reason the family has the right to sue the nanny for breach of contract.

Should I provide the nanny with a detailed list of what her job entails?

The job details should be outlined for the nanny when she is hired. Since taking care of the children is the top priority all the details should be outlined clearly.

A nanny's first day is typically full of excitement and would want to impress her boss. She may go overboard in making the house look spotless. Now two things can occur: The boss comes in and is shocked to see the house put together and her child is well taken care of. Now the nanny is expected to do the same thing every day which leaves the nanny in a bind because there are times, she is not able to have the time to do it all and wonders to herself, what have I started.

The other dilemma that can occur is you come home, and things are not put in their rightful place and now you are annoyed and angry. This is why a list is important, so the nanny knows what is expected from her, so she does not have to guess what you want.

How will you keep clear boundaries for the Nanny/housekeeper?

A nanny and a housekeeper are two entirely two different positions and should be treated as such. Light housekeeping is generally expected in the nanny's job from washing the

dishes which have been used by the children or picking up toys and straightening up the living and the bedroom of the children.

Hiring a nanny to take care of your children and a household is not a very wise decision.

How will you handle credit card/ petty cash?

Hiring a nanny to fill in when you are not there is extremely helpful. For your nanny to be able to take the children or to do fun activities such as the park, or to go get some ice cream on a hot day would bring a smile to any child.

For these little moments it is good to have some petty cash for your nanny to carry with her for these moments and not to rely on your nanny to have cash of her own on hand. Another issue could arise if your child needs to unexpectedly have to go to the doctor and you are not able to take him/her. It would be convenient if your nanny had a credit card from you with her name on it to pay for the doctor bill and you would not have wait to take the child in the next day. In the event a credit card is used there should be   receipts provided to show what was spent on the credit card.

What is the price for overnight care?

The overnight stay should be really clarified explicitly since it beyond a normal workday If my child is sleeping, the nanny isn't required to do anything so why should I pay her to just sleep at my house. One must take into consideration you are paying her for her time even though she is sleeping over while your child is also sleeping. The nanny cannot go out with her friends that night or do her usually things which she is a custom doing or even sleeping in her own bed.

. For instance if the nanny usually gets paid $20 an hour during her regular shift which is 8am to 8pm while the child is awake, then while child is a sleep, after 8pm the pay is cut in half which is $10 a hour so you are paying $10 an hour from 8pm to 7am which is 11 hours at $10 an hour which comes to $110 or you could both agree on a set price like an extra $100 for the night.

Why are you hiring a nanny in the first place?

The number one reason why you would want to hire a more permanent nanny is for stability for your child. If you are a mom who knows your job would demand a lot of your time, you need to have someone who you can depend on to take care of your children for those long hours at work or unexpected calls early in the morning which were not planned. You need someone who is flexible, and the children are comfortable with and know.

Be familiar with the laws governing pay and benefits for domestic workers in your state.

What is the nanny's driving record?

If your nanny will be driving the children around to and from school, requiring a clean driving record is not unreasonable but no driver is perfect. The nanny should be forthcoming if she gets a ticket so you can make an informed decision. She should also disclose any DUI or speeding tickets.

What should be in a nanny contract?

A nanny contract should reflect what has been discussed and agreed upon with the employer and the nanny. The contract should have the date when the nanny starts. 2) your responsibilities 3) holidays 4) mileage reimbursement 5) work hours 6) overtime pay 7) vacation 8) confidentiality agreement 9) pay increase 10) sick days 11) termination etc.

The break-up: How will you handle termination?

Terminating one from a job position is not easy for both parties, the employer and the employee. It's especially hard for the employer to let go of her nanny if she has been with the family for a number of years and the children genuinely loves her. No matter the reason for the termination, there is no easy way going about it, it literally feels like a break- up on both sides especially for the nanny if the news is unexpected.

Letting go of your nanny can be very hard, but it does not have to leave completely on a bad note. It all depends on the circumstances surrounding the termination. You can offer the nanny, 1) A letter reference for her next job, 2) A two week notice from the date of termination, 3) One or two months of pay depending on how generous you want to be.

If the nanny would like to keep in touch with the family especially the kids, it will be up to you to use your discretion if that would be ok.

How do you feel about the nanny being on time.?

Time management is crucial for the workforce as for the home but not everyone has this particular area mastered as well as others. A nanny should be someone you can depend on to take care of your children, the household and being on time.

Giving several stern warnings is sufficient, you could say this is the second time you have been late if this happens again, I will have no choice but to let you go. This would hopefully let the nanny know you mean business and should take the proper precautions arriving to work a little bit earlier than what is recommended.

If you currently have a nanny and have mixed feelings about whether or not you should keep her in your household, here are five warning signs to watch out for. Any one of these should be cause enough for you to give pause about keeping your live-in nanny.

- Your child seems apprehensive around your live-in nanny and is reluctant to go to her.
- You make repeated requests to your nanny, and she doesn't follow them.
- Your child seems prone to getting into accidents with your nanny, signaling a potential lack of attention.
- Your live-in nanny criticizes the way you raise your child.
- Your live-in nanny seems reluctant to share information about her day with your child or seems to be giving you contradictory stories.

- See more at:
http://www.nannies4hire.com/tips/1046-live-in-nannies.htm#sthash.56JcTyvc.dpuf

Our Beloved Natasha

Natasha Christine Ross was born February 8, 1976, in London, England. Natasha graduated from Rincon High School in Tucson, Arizona. Natasha relocated to California over twenty-five years ago and went on to obtain college and university degrees. She received an Associate degree in Child Development from Santa Monica College, California and her Bachelors in Small Business and Entrepreneurship from the University of Phoenix, in California. At the time of her death, she was working on two books slated to be published early this year. Natasha was also a teacher's aide at her church, Valley Vineyard Church.

Natasha loved the Lord, loved people but had a passion and compassion for children. She spent most of her adult life working with children and families. Natasha has never met a stranger; she had the ability to engage with everyone. She had a great personality, an infectious laughter and a smile that lit up the room.

Natasha was a hard worker; she was quite involved in the churches she attended as well as her community. Natasha was also very involved in mentoring young adults and children. She was loved and appreciated by so many people, and she is sorely missed.

Natasha's Nanny Book is the result of the efforts of the family that she worked for, and the knowledge garnered from being a nanny. Many people thought that she was wasting her life as a nanny, but she saw it as her calling. Her love and passion for this work and the families that she impacted brought her pure joy. Natasha was a very giving person and wanted to share her experiences with other women who chose to venture into becoming nannies. Natasha is indebted to the families she worked for because through their trust in her to care for their families, she is now able to pass

on her experience, this incredible legacy to others, even after her death.

This book is being published posthumously with the help of her family and friends.